The Basic Skills Agency

LITERACY & NUMERACY

WHAT ADULTS CAN AND CAN'T DO

There's considerable evidence that large numbers of adults have difficulties with reading and writing and with basic maths. The latest estimate is 7 million in this country. This is a worrying and shocking fact and should concern us all. Even though this country has a long tradition of compulsory education, we still fail to give some people the basic skills they will need for adult life.

It's good to say things are improving. Action in our schools is reducing the number of children with such poor basic skills that they can't cope when they go to secondary school. This in turn is also reducing the number of young people leaving school with limited literacy and numeracy skills. And action is also being taken to help adults with poor basic skills to improve these skills to an acceptable standard.

However, it's important to be clear that poor basic skills are rarely about an adult being entirely illiterate or innumerate. We don't have many illiterate or innumerate adults in the UK. What we have are lots of people who can't cope with the level of written information most of us face daily and can't use numbers well enough in a world of figures, charts, graphs and statistics.

This booklet sets out what adults can and can't do. It's a simple account, based on extensive testing and assessment over a number of years, of tasks people found straightforward or difficult if not impossible. It doesn't show a nation of illiterates and innumerates; rather it shows what poor skills mean at the beginning of the 21st century.

Alan Wells OBE
Director, The Basic Skills Agency

KR39754

Published October 2000

ISBN 1 85990 129 8

Design: Studio 21

LITERACY

Dear Pat,

As I am going to be late home from work today I would be very grateful if you could buy some items for me on your regular trip to the supermarket. I shall need:

a large loaf of sliced brown bread
a jar of marmalade
a packet of cornflakes
1 pound of apples
1 packet (1 kg) of basmati rice
2 small plain yoghurts

I enclose £10.00 to cover the cost of these items.

I hope to see you at about 9 o'clock this evening.

Thank you very much for your kindness.

Jo

Q. What does Jo want Pat to do for her?

A. To do some shopping/buy some items in the supermarket

98% ✓

2% ✗

Q. Why does she ask Pat to do the shopping?

A. Because she is going to be home late

94% ✓

6% ✗

Q. At what time does Jo expect to return home?

A. About nine o'clock (this evening)

97% ✓ *

2% ✗ *

*Where percentages do not total 100 this is the result of respondents not answering the question.

HOW TO GROW YOUR PLANTS

1 Fill pots with soil. Press soil down until it feels firm.

2 Tear off your seed stick.

3 Push it into centre of pot to line marked. Lightly press down soil.

4 Water lightly (don't over-water).

5 Put in warm and light space.

6 Pinch out the weakest seedlings to allow strongest to grow on.

Q. When you fill the pot with soil what should the soil feel like after you have pressed it down?

A. Firm

Q. Which seedlings should be allowed to continue to grow?

A. The strongest seedlings

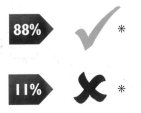

SPECIAL DELIVERY

BY AIR MAIL
par avion

Royal Mail

URGENT

FRAGILE–Handle with Care

THIS WAY UP

Q. Can you tell me which label would be put on a parcel that is easily damaged?

A. Fragile – Handle with Care

Q. What label would show that the parcel was sent by air?

A. Air Mail

501 PLUMBERS

Achilles Plumbing Services
35 Paynes Walk Hammersmith W6...................020-8520 3012

A D L S Plumbing & Heating
4 St John's Terr W10......................................020-8450 6882

ADVANCED CONSULTANTS

*See our advertisement
adjacent to Fingertip Fact
Page 419*

020-7222 0282

982 Eastern Ave Ilford Essex

A J & P PLUMBING & HEATING ENGINEERS

★ *See Our Larger
Advertisement Page 431*

313 Lyle Road SW6...020-7610 1616

ALBERT A. BLISSETT LTD

Industry Established 15 Years

Corgi Reg/Plumbing/Heating

For Emergencies 0860 251378

020-8451 1658

30 Ilex Rd London NW10

ALL LONDON PLUMBING SERVICES

★ *See Our Larger
Advertisement Page 439*

108 Plough Rd Battersea London SW11........020-7738 0800

Ambassador Plumbing
177-179 Proed St W2.....................................020-7724 4434

ANDERSON & SONS

★ *See Our Larger
Advertisement Page 440*

25 Filmer Rd Fulham SW6.............................020-7381 3784

The Thomson Directory – complete with
National Dialling Codes

---

24 HOUR EMERGENCY PLUMBING

- BURST PIPES
- BOILER BREAKDOWN
- TANKS & CYLINDERS
- NO CALL OUT CHARGE (BEFORE 8pm)
- BLOCKED DRAINS TOILETS & SINKS
- ALL PLUMBING WORK
- FREE ESTIMATES
- WORK GUARANTEED

*WE ARE A LONG ESTABLISHED
FAMILY FIRM, OFFERING A
PROMPT & RELIABLE SERVICE
AT AFFORDABLE PRICES*

ASSETT PLUMBING

DAY: 020-8894 2670
EVE: 020-8561 6803

For consumer, health and general
advice, see Helplines in the
Thomson Information pages

B.S.B Heating & Plumbing Contractors
Central Heating Installation and Repairs
53 Aldridge Rd Villas W11................................020-7229 3731

BUCKINGHAM S.F. & SONS LTD

★ *See Our Larger
Advertisement Page 440*

56 Wedmore Gardens London N19...............020-7281 4536

Building & Plumbing The Wright Way
59a Inglethorpe St SW6.......................................020-7381 9527

Central Plumbing Service
414a Edgware Rd W2..020-7723 5300
Collins A 26 Bourne Terr W2.............................020-7289 3898

CO-OPERATIVE PLUMBING

★ *See Our Larger
Advertisement Page 441*

40-41 MARYLEBONE HIGH ST MARYLEBONE W1.........020-766 2611

Dent & Hellyer Ltd
85 Bell St NW1...020-7724 7234

DRAINWISE

★ *See Our Larger
Advertisement Page 441*

Conduit Business Centre 1A Conduit Rd
Plumstead London SE 18.................................020-8855 5525

DRISCOLL & CROWLEY

★ *See Our Larger
Advertisement Page 435*

496a Barking Rd London E13............................020-7515 1217

E. G. Woods Plumbing
105 Oliphant St W10.....................................020-8969 9999

EMBASSY PLUMBING SERVICES

★ *See Our Larger
Advertisement Page 442*

414a Edware Rd W2...020-7724 2546

Use the colour Thomson Information pages

Q. Can you find a plumber you could call at any time of the day or night?

A. Assett Plumbing

Q. What is the telephone number of the firm called 'All London Plumbing Services'?

A. 020 7738 0800

The Stowaway Cat

WHISKY the cat had only planned to curl up for a quick snooze after a night on the tiles in Louisville, Kentucky. She ended up nursing a bad hangover after spending thirty days in a used whisky barrel while crossing the Atlantic Ocean by ship.

The young black and white cat survived without food by licking the dregs from the wooden barrel. When she walked unsteadily into the whisky distillery in Keith, Scotland, she was very much the worse for wear.

"She was struggling to get to her feet, not just through lack of food, but because she would also have been somewhat affected by the whisky," said company boss John Watson.

The police, who were called to look into this unlawful entry, said cat stowaways are usually destroyed. But the company decided to spare what was left of Whisky the cat's nine lives.

"It seemed the only decent thing to do after all she has been through. It's amazing that she's still alive."

Whisky is now serving out her time in a cattery. She had lost weight during the journey by ship but was able to get vital nourishment from the whisky dregs.

Adapted from report by Angelia Johnson, *The Guardian*, 17.6.93

Q. How did Whisky survive without food?

A. She licked the dregs from the barrel.

93% ✓ *

6% ✗ *

Q. What are we told in the newspaper extract about the cat's condition when she walked into the distillery in Scotland?

A. She was very much the worse for wear.

68% ✓ *

31% ✗ *

Q. Where is Whisky now?

A. In a cattery (or home for stray cats) or in Scotland

93% ✓

7% ✗

MUESLI AND HONEY COOKIES

60g (2oz/2 tablespoons) clear honey
60g (2oz/¼ cup) unsalted butter
125g (4oz) plain (dark) chocolate, chopped
250g (8oz/2 cups) muesli

1 Butter a shallow tin measuring 27.5 x 17.5cm (11 x 7in). Line base with non-stick paper. Melt honey, butter and chocolate together in a large bowl placed over a saucepan of gently simmering water.

2 Reserve 30g (1oz/¼ cup) of muesli. Stir remaining muesli into honey mixture. Spread in prepared tin, smoothing top with the back of a spoon.

3 Sprinkle reserved muesli evenly on top, then press gently into surface of mixture. Refrigerate for 1-2 hours until mixture is firmly set.

4 Carefuly remove muesli slab from tin and remove paper. Cut in half lengthwise, then into 4 widthwise, to make 8 squares. Cut each square in half to make 2 triangles.

Makes 16.

Q. How much honey do you need to make the cookies?

A. 60g or 2oz or 2 tablespoons

Q. How long should you keep the mixture in the refrigerator?

A. 1 – 2 hours

Q. How many cookies does this recipe make?

A. 16

Panex *Junior*

Soluble Paracetamol Tablets

How much to use

DISSOLVE TABLETS IN WATER	
Age	No. of Tablets
6-12 years	2 to 4
1-6 years	1 to 2

For children under 5 years PANEX Infants is available from your chemist. Not to be used by children under 1 year.

KEEP OUT OF REACH OF CHILDREN

PANEX Junior Soluble Tablets have been specially made to give fast, effective relief from the pain or fever of Headache, Toothache, Colds, Flu and general aches and pains.

Sugar Free	✓
Gentle on Stomach	✓
Pleasant Fruity Taste	✓

How often

Wait 4 hours before giving another dose of this medicine. Do not give more than 4 doses in 24 hours. DO NOT EXCEED THE STATED DOSE.

Caution

If you are giving your child other medicines, consult your doctor before giving this product. Do not give any other medicine containing paracetamol within 4 hours of giving this product. If symptoms persist, consult your doctor. Do not give for more than 3 days without seeing your doctor. In case of accidental overdose, see your doctor immediately.

Contains Paracetamol

Each tablet contains 120mg of paracetamol PH. Eur. in a fizzy base. Contains saccharin.

Made in UK

ch **Colefield & Hastings,** Westfield Lane, Birmingham

9 00259 03795 6

Q. How many tablets should a three-year-old be given as a dose?

A. 1 or 2 (or 1 to 2)

 *

 *

Q. How long should you wait before giving a child a second dose of this medicine?

A. 4 hours

 *

 *

Q. Should the tablets be dissolved in water?

A. Yes

Q. 'I want to apply for the job.' Please spell <u>apply</u>.

A. APPLY

90% ✓

10% ✗

Q. 'I wish to complain about the service.' Please spell <u>complain</u>.

A. COMPLAIN

92% ✓

8% ✗

Q. 'I am writing to you about the vacancy.' Please spell <u>writing</u>.

A. WRITING

88% ✓

12% ✗

Q. 'I am unhappy because you are not coming to visit.' Please spell <u>because</u>.

A. BECAUSE

95% ✓

5% ✗

NUMERACY

68p
each

45p
each

Q. You have bought me a loaf of bread and two tins of soup. How much money do I owe you?

A. £1.58

80% ✓ *

19% ✗ *

> Give the following coins to the respondent: 1 × 50p, 2 × 20p, 2 × 5p, 2 × 2p, 2 × 1p.

Q. Here is £2.00 to cover some shopping that cost £1.58. Please give me the change you owe me.

> Hand over two £1.00 coins.

A. 42p

88% ✓ *

11% ✗ *

Hazledene & Co.

The Dene, Almsford, Hampshire.

Interview Details:

Interview time:	11.30
Please arrive by:	11.15

Hazledean & Co. are a 10 minute walk from Almsford Railway Station.

South East Trains — Timetable

Morton to Turnerstone — Mon-Fri

Morton	10.17	10.37	10.57	11.17
Graves End	10.21	10.41	11.01	11.21
Newgate	10.32	10.52	11.12	11.32
Appleby	10.40	11.00	11.20	11.40
Meadstone	10.49	11.09	11.29	11.49
Almsford	10.55	11.15	11.35	11.55
Turnerstone	11.01	11.21	11.41	12.01

Turnerstone to Morton — Mon-Fri

Turnerstone	12.24	12.59	13.34	13.59
Almsford	12.30	13.05	13.40	14.05
Meadstone	12.36	13.11	13.46	14.11
Appleby	12.45	13.20	13.55	14.20
Newgate	12.53	13.28	14.03	14.28
Graves End	13.04	13.39	14.14	14.39
Morton	13.08	13.43	14.18	14.43

Q. Imagine that you have an interview for a job. You need to work out which train to take.

The interview is at 11.30. You want to arrive early at 11.15.

There is a ten-minute walk from the station to the company. You will take the train from Newgate Station.

Work out which train you need so that you arrive *at the company* by 11.15?

A. 10.32 from Newgate

Q. The interview finishes at 12.30. Which train would you take home?

A. 13.05

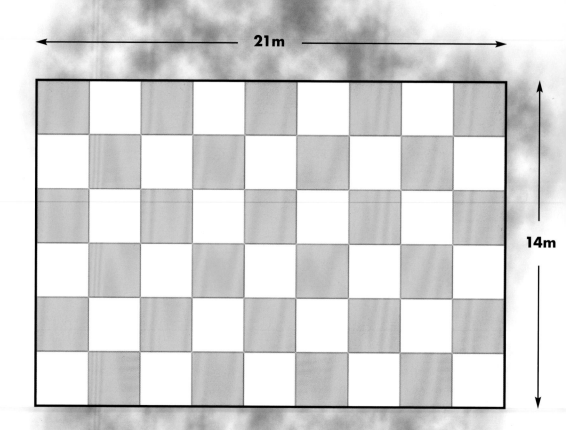

21m

14m

Q. Here is a diagram of a room. The length and width of the room has been measured. Please calculate the floor area of the room.

A. 294 square metres

21ft

14ft

Q. Here is a diagram of a room. The length and width of the room has been measured. Please calculate the floor area of the room.

A. 294 square feet

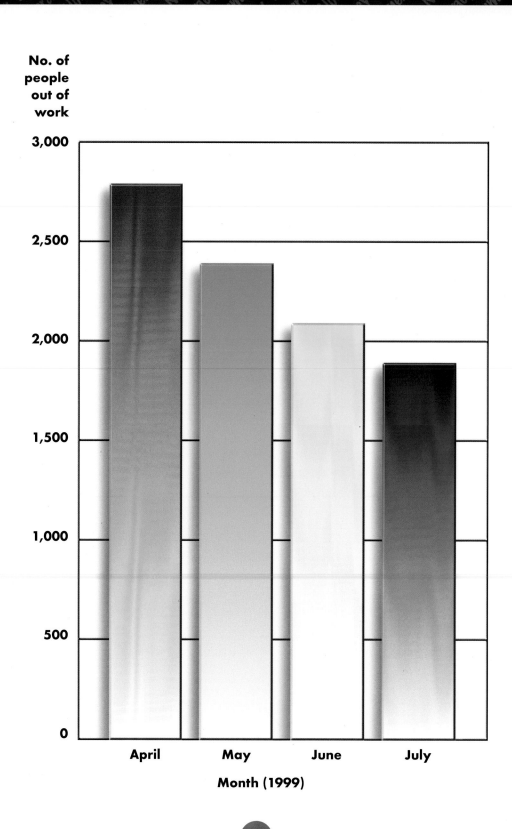

No. of people out of work

Month (1999)

Q. About how many people were out of work in May?

A. About 2,400 (or any answer between 2,350 and 2,450)

 *

 *

Q. Which month had the highest unemployment?

A. April

Q. How many light bulbs are in stock?

A. 40

Q. How many plates are in stock?

A. 25

2 Videos
£2.50 each

Takeaway
Pizza
£19.66

Fresh
PIZZA
Baked!

Hand the respondent a calculator, rough paper and a pen.

Q. Imagine you and five friends order some takeaway pizza while watching videos.

Two videos were hired for the evening. Each video costs £2.50 for the evening. The pizza cost £19.66 in total.

Work out the total cost for the videos and pizza.

A. £24.66

Q. Work out how much each person has to pay.

Remind the respondent that there are six of you in total.

A. £4.11

 *

 *

STANDARD
60 watt bulbs
Average life
1000 HOURS

STANDARD
Pack of two
99p
60ʷ

DOUBLE LIFE
Pack of two
£1.75
60ʷ

DOUBLE LIFE
60 watt bulbs
Average life
2000 HOURS

LONG LIFE
60 watt bulbs
Average life
4000 HOURS

LONG LIFE
Pack of two
£3.99
60ʷ

Q. Use the information on this sheet to decide which type of light bulb is the best value for money.

A. Double Life 60 watt bulbs

Q. Why is that type of light bulb the best value for money?

A. Because it is the cheapest for each hour of light/you get more hours of light for your money.

Anytown Bank Loan Rate Table

	Loans Under £2,500 APR 21.9%			Loans of £2,500 to £4,900 APR 19.9%			Loans of £5,000 and over APR 16.9%			
	£100*	£500	£2,000	£2,500	£100*	£500*	£5,000	£10,000	£100*	£500*
12 MONTHS										
Total to repay £	111.24	555.96	2223.60	2755.08	110.16	551.04	5436.12	10872.12	108.72	543.60
Monthly repayment £	9.26	46.32	185.30	229.59	9.18	45.92	453.01	906.01	9.06	45.30
24 MONTHS										
Total to repay £	122.16	611.04	2443.68	3005.04	120.24	600.96	5859.84	11719.68	117.12	586.08
Monthly repayment £	5.09	25.46	101.82	125.21	5.01	25.04	244.16	488.32	4.88	24.42
36 MONTHS										
Total to repay £	133.92	669.24	2676.96	3268.44	130.68	653.76	6303.96	12607.92	126.00	630.36
Monthly repayment £	3.71	18.59	74.36	90.79	3.63	18.16	175.11	350.22	3.50	17.51
48 MONTHS										
Total to repay £	145.92	730.56	2923.20	3545.76	141.60	708.96	6768.00	13536.00	135.36	676.80
Monthly repayment £	3.04	15.22	60.90	73.87	2.95	14.77	141.00	282.00	2.82	14.10
60 MONTHS										
Total to repay £	159.00	795.60	3181.80	3835.80	153.60	767.40	7251.60	14503.20	145.20	725.40
Monthly repayment £	2.65	13.26	53.03	63.93	2.55	12.79	120.86	241.72	2.42	12.09

*Shown for calculation purposes only

British Savings Bank Loan Rate Table

LOAN	APR	60 month term		48 month term		36 month term		24 month term		12 month term	
		Monthly Repayment	Total Payable	Monthly Repayment	Total Payable	Monthly Repayment	Total Payable	Monthly Repayment	Total Payable	Monthly Repayment	Total Payable
1000		26.01	1560.60	29.97	1438.56	36.72	1321.92	50.47	1211.28	92.22	1106.64
1500	20.9%	39.02	2341.20	44.95	2157.60	55.08	1982.88	75.71	1817.04	138.33	1659.96
2000		52.02	3121.20	59.94	2877.12	73.44	2643.84	100.94	2422.56	184.44	2213.28
2500		62.72	3763.20	72.70	3489.60	89.68	3228.48	124.13	2979.12	228.53	2742.36
3000	18.9%	75.26	4515.60	87.24	4187.52	107.61	3873.96	148.96	3575.04	274.24	3290.88
4000		100.35	6021.00	116.33	5583.84	143.48	5165.28	198.61	4766.64	365.65	4387.80
5000		125.44	7526.40	145.41	6979.68	179.35	6456.60	248.26	5958.24	457.06	5484.72

Hand the respondent a calculator, rough paper and a pen.

Q. You are going to borrow £2,500. Use the information on the sheet to decide whether to borrow the money from Anytown Bank or the British Savings Bank, if you want to pay it back over two years.

Point to the APR interest rates on the tables and say 'these columns show the interest rates'.

A. British Savings Bank loan

Q. If you wanted to borrow more money, £5,000, which bank would you choose? You are going to pay the money back over four years.

A. Anytown Bank

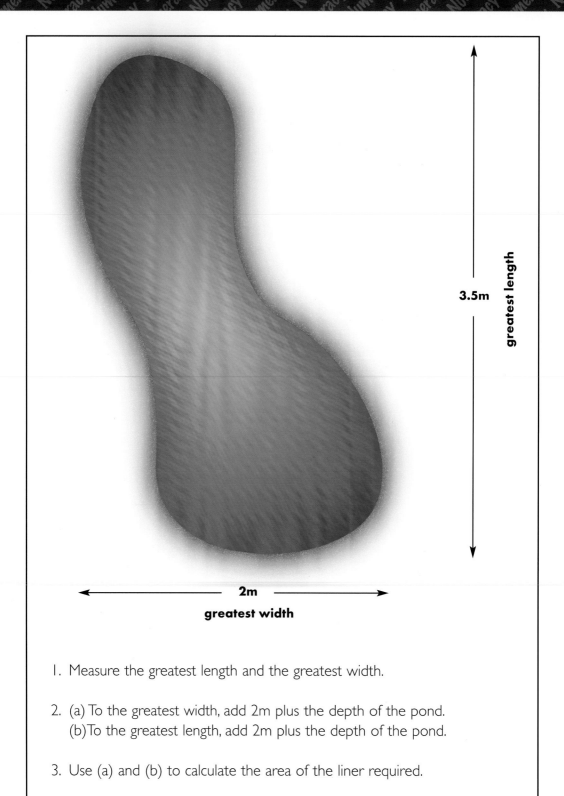

3.5m — greatest length

2m — greatest width

1. Measure the greatest length and the greatest width.

2. (a) To the greatest width, add 2m plus the depth of the pond.
   (b) To the greatest length, add 2m plus the depth of the pond.

3. Use (a) and (b) to calculate the area of the liner required.

Q. Imagine that you are going to dig a pond in the garden. The pond will have to be lined with PVC, which is priced in pence per square metre.

On this sheet is a diagram of the pond showing measurements. The sheet gives you the instructions for working out the amount of pond liner required. You must use the instructions given to work out your answer.

Calculate the area of liner you will need for this pond. Assume that the pond is going to be two metres deep.

A. 45 square metres

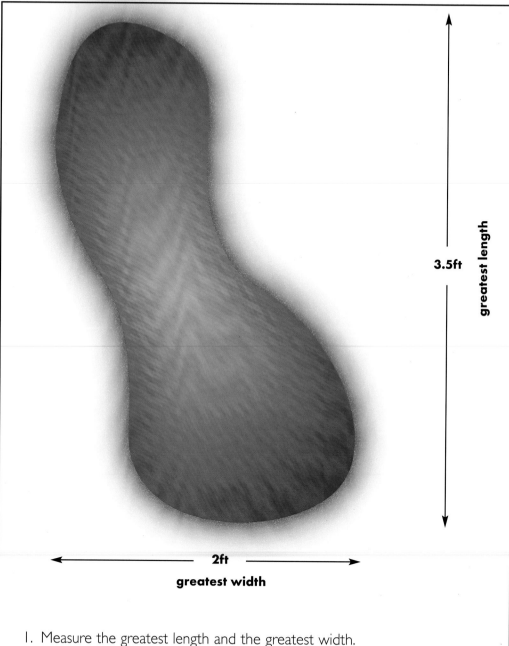

3.5ft greatest length

2ft
greatest width

1. Measure the greatest length and the greatest width.

2. (a) To the greatest width, add 2ft plus the depth of the pond.
   (b) To the greatest length, add 2ft plus the depth of the pond.

3. Use (a) and (b) to calculate the area of the liner required.

Q. Imagine that you are going to dig a pond in the garden. The pond will have to be lined with PVC, which is priced in pence per square foot.

On this sheet is a diagram of the pond showing measurements. The sheet gives you the instructions for working out the amount of pond liner required. You must use the instructions given to work out your answer.

Calculate the area of liner you will need for this pond. Assume that the pond is going to be two feet deep.

A. 45 square feet

DEPARTMENT	1993 (£m)	1994 (£m)
Education	23.73	24.28
Housing	6.24	5.96
Cleansing	2.16	2.87
Fire	1.99	2.31
Police	8.80	10.34
Ambulance	2.85	3.02
Other	6.50	10.25
Total	52.27	58.85

Q. What was the 1993 Education spending, to the nearest million pounds?

A. £24 million

Q. Which department spent nearly six million pounds in 1994?

A. Housing